LOOKING INSIDE THE

HUMAN
BODY

BY EMMA HUDDLESTON

Published by The Child's World®
1980 Lookout Drive • Mankato, MN 56003-1705
800-599-READ • www.childsworld.com

Photographs ©: Shutterstock Images, cover, 1, 2; Alfazet Chronicles/iStockphoto, 5; Ruslan Dashinsky/iStockphoto, 6; iStockphoto, 8, 11, 13, 16, 21, 24; Hank Grebe/iStockphoto, 12; Anatomy Insider/Shutterstock Images, 15; Phonlamai Photo/iStockphoto, 17; Alex Mit/iStockphoto, 19

ISBN 9781503835191
LCCN 2019943114

Printed in the United States of America

ABOUT THE AUTHOR

Emma Huddleston is a children's book author. She lives in Minnesota with her husband. She enjoys learning about the world in which we live while she writes.

TABLE OF CONTENTS

CHAPTER ONE

Cells and Tissues

The human body is made up of trillions of cells. A cell is the building block of living things. It is tiny. The only way to see a cell is with a microscope. More than 200 types of cells work together in the human body.

Cells make up tissues. Tissues are groups of cells that work together. Different types of tissues do different jobs. For example, the brain is made of nerve cells. These cells make up nerve tissue. Nerves send messages throughout the brain and to the body.

Cells and tissues make up all parts of the human body. The human body has four main layers. Skin is the outer layer. Underneath are the muscles, organs, and skeleton. These layers overlap and work together.

Layers of the Body

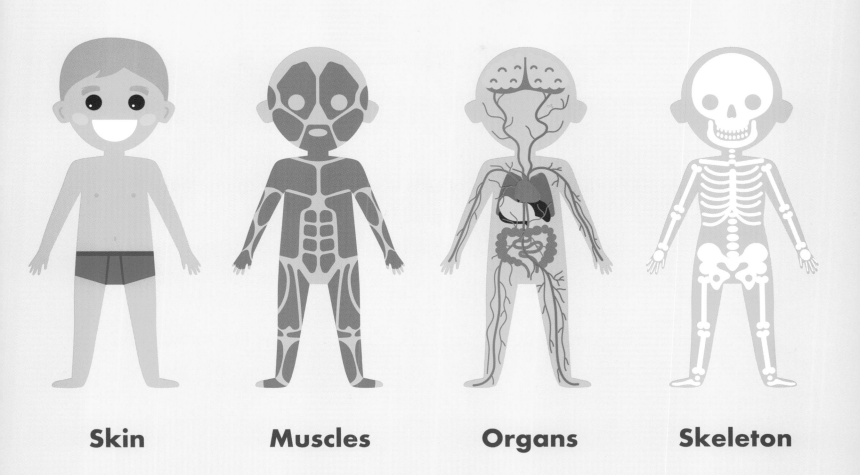

Skin   Muscles   Organs   Skeleton

Fingernails grow faster than toenails.

CHAPTER TWO

Skin

Skin is the body's outer layer. It is a protective covering. It holds everything inside. Skin has nerves in it. The nerves make skin **sensitive**. Nerves feel tiny movements. They feel whether something is hot or cold. They send all these messages to the brain. Some nerves surround the bases of hairs.

Nails grow out of the skin. They are hard and flat. They protect the tips of fingers and toes. Nails grow all the time. It takes about three months for a whole nail to replace itself.

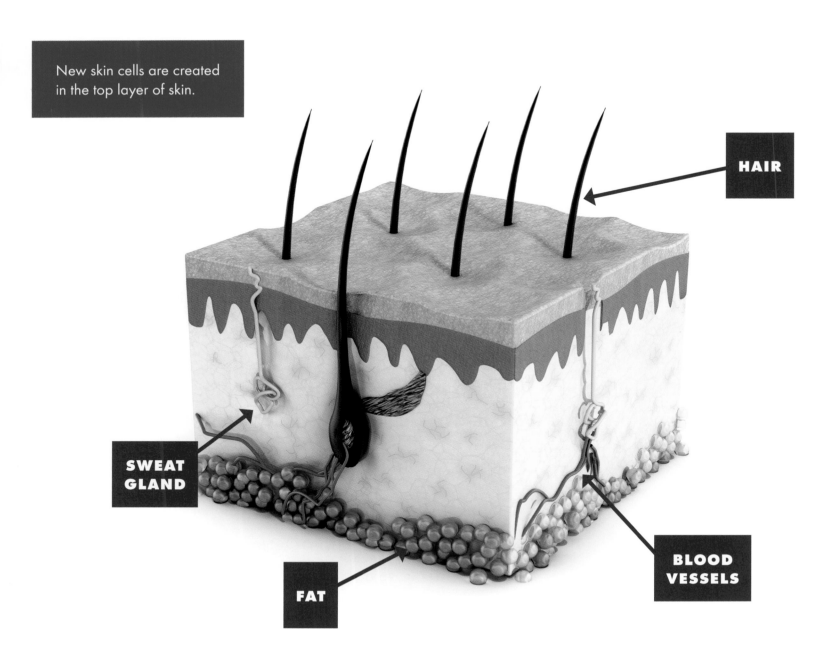

New skin cells are created in the top layer of skin.

HAIR

SWEAT GLAND

FAT

BLOOD VESSELS

Skin itself has three layers. The inner layer is fatty. It supplies **nutrients** to the layers above. It also keeps the body warm. The middle layer is the thickest part of the skin. It can stretch out and snap back into place. **Blood vessels** are here. Hair grows out of this layer. Sweat **glands** are in this layer. Sweat helps keep the body at a regular temperature.

The top layer of skin is thicker in some areas than in others. For example, the palms of the hands and the soles of the feet are thick. Those areas need to be tough. Some cells on the skin's top layer are dead. Dead cells flake off the body.

CHAPTER THREE

Muscles

The muscle layer is underneath the skin. Muscle is a type of tissue that **contracts**. Muscle produces movement. Movement allows people to do daily activities. Without movement, people would not be able to eat, walk, or breathe.

There are three main types of muscle. Most muscle in the human body is skeletal. Skeletal muscle attaches to bones. It moves the body. People are aware of their skeletal muscles. People control when these muscles move and what movements they make. For example, calves are skeletal muscles in the lower legs. They let people rise up on their toes.

The human body has more than 600 skeletal muscles.

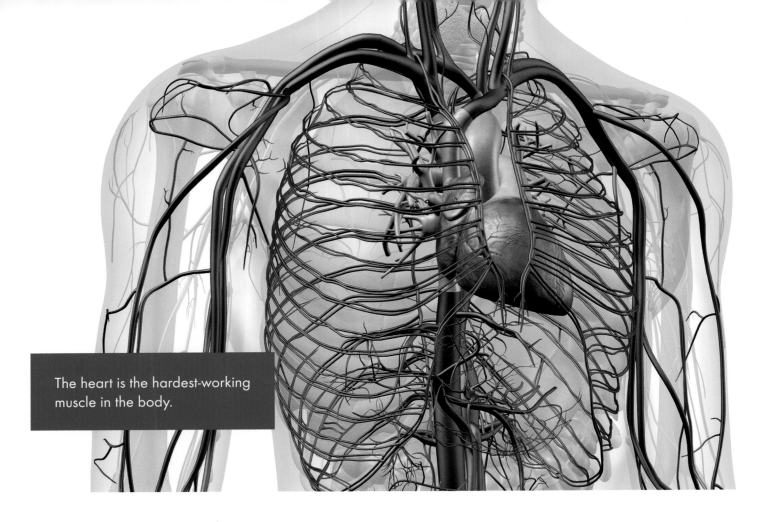

The heart is the hardest-working muscle in the body.

The second type of muscle is cardiac muscle. It is only found in the heart. Cardiac muscle makes the heart pump blood. Cardiac muscle works on its own. People cannot control when their heart beats.

Smooth muscle is the third type of muscle. It lines organs, blood vessels, and skin. It helps organs do many jobs. For example, smooth muscle in the stomach contracts to help break down food. Like cardiac muscle, smooth muscle cannot be controlled. Smooth muscle contracts more slowly than skeletal muscle. It also uses less energy to contract.

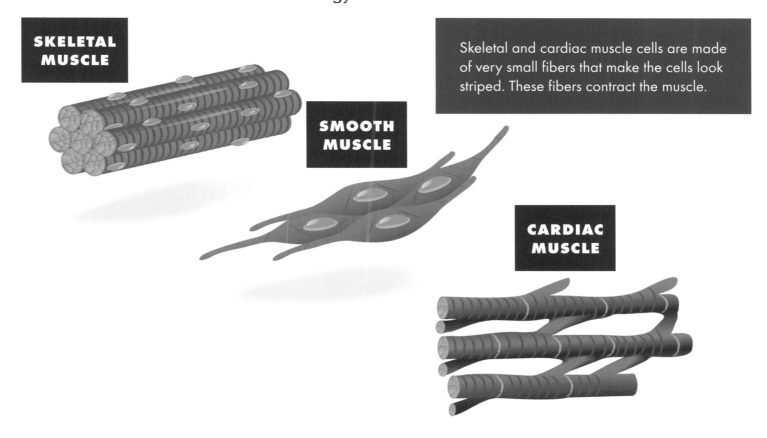

SKELETAL MUSCLE

SMOOTH MUSCLE

CARDIAC MUSCLE

Skeletal and cardiac muscle cells are made of very small fibers that make the cells look striped. These fibers contract the muscle.

CHAPTER FOUR

Organs

Organs are found throughout the body. They are made of groups of tissues. Each organ has its own purpose.

Most organs are internal. They are inside the body. People cannot see them. The brain is one of many internal organs. It is located in the head. It is made of 100 billion nerve cells. An adult brain weighs about 3.3 pounds (1.5 kg). The brain controls the whole body. The stomach and intestines are also internal organs. The stomach breaks down food. The intestines are long tubes. They take in nutrients from the food.

Some organs are external. They are partly outside the body. The eyes, ears, nose, and tongue are external organs. People use them to see, hear, smell, and taste.

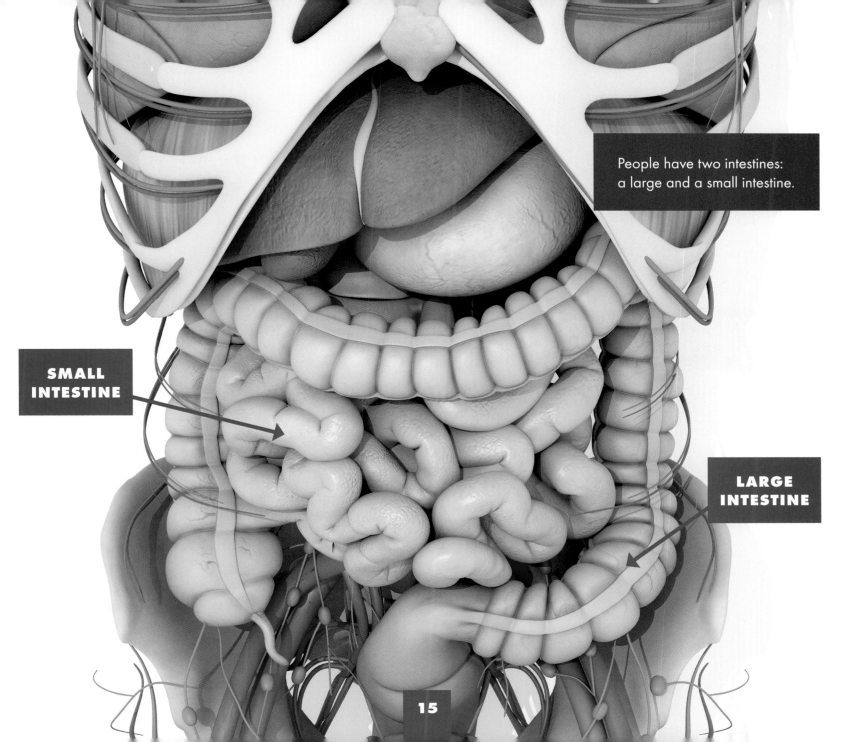

People have two intestines: a large and a small intestine.

SMALL INTESTINE

LARGE INTESTINE

A group of organs makes up an organ system. Organs in a system work together. The human body has nine major organ systems. Organ systems help the body accomplish different tasks. One system helps the body breathe. The main organ in this system is the lungs. Lungs pull air into the body. They collect oxygen from the air. The oxygen goes into the blood. Lungs then push out the air the body does not need.

Lungs have tubes in them that direct air.

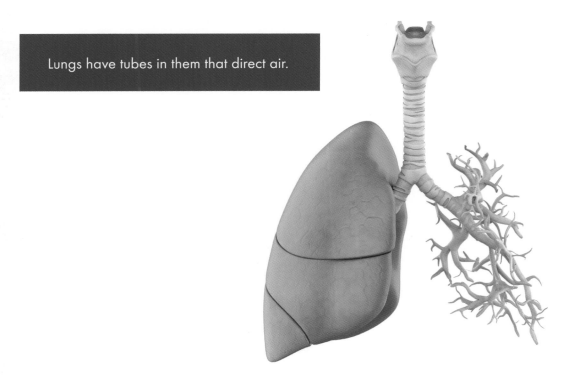

Another system moves blood throughout the body. The main organ of this system is the heart. It pushes blood through blood vessels. These carry the blood. One system removes waste from the body. The kidneys are part of this system. Kidneys are shaped like beans. The body has two kidneys. They clean the blood.

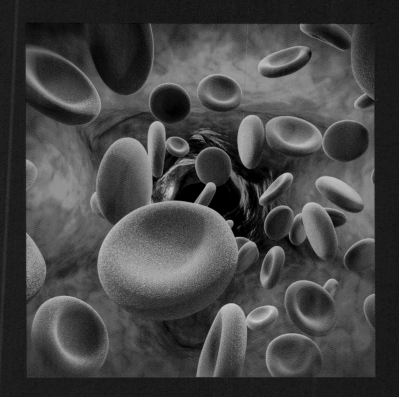

Blood

Blood is both a tissue and a liquid. It is made of cells that float in a liquid. Blood reaches every part of the body. It carries oxygen and nutrients to the body's cells. It takes waste away from those cells. Cells cannot survive without the flow of blood.

CHAPTER FIVE

Skeleton

The skeleton is the base of the body. It is made of 206 bones. Everything in the body is built around the skeleton.

The skeleton has two main parts. One part supports and protects the body. This part includes the spine, skull, and rib cage. The spine is made of many little bones. It runs down the center of the back. It protects the spinal cord. The spinal cord sends messages from the brain to the rest of the body. The skull and rib cage protect organs such as the brain and heart.

The second part is made for motion. It includes the hand, foot, arm, and leg bones. The largest and strongest bones in the body are the thigh bones.

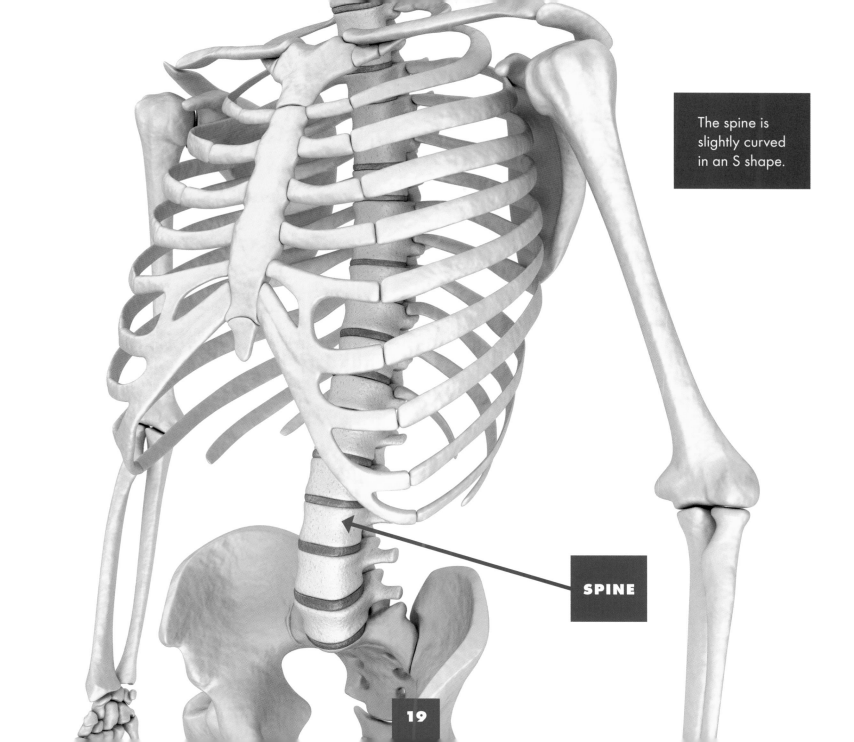

The spine is slightly curved in an S shape.

SPINE

Bones connect at joints. There are different types of joints. The names of the joints describe how they work. One example is a hinge joint. Hinges bend in one direction. Elbows are hinge joints. Another example is a joint that has a **socket**. This is called a ball-and-socket joint. A ball rolls in a socket. It can move more freely in all directions. Hips are ball-and-socket joints.

The space between bones is cushioned by a padding tissue called **cartilage**. Bones are connected by **ligaments**. Muscles connect to bones with **tendons**. Ligaments and tendons hold the body together. They are thicker and stronger than other tissues.

The human body is made of a combination of layers. Each layer is important. The body's layers work together every day to keep a person alive.

FAST FACTS

- The cell is the basic building block of the human body. Different cells make up different tissues.

- The human body is made up of trillions of cells.

- Skin has three layers. The skin protects the body.

- Hair and nails grow out of skin.

- Muscles contract to produce movement.

- The three types of muscle are skeletal, cardiac, and smooth.

- Organs are groups of tissues that have a purpose.

- Organs work together in systems. Organ systems help the body breathe, move blood, remove waste, and more.

- The skeleton protects and supports the body.

- The skeleton is made of 206 bones.

GLOSSARY

blood vessels (BLUHD VESS-uhlz) Blood vessels are narrow tubes where blood flows. Blood vessels reach all parts of the body.

cartilage (KAR-tuh-lij) Cartilage is a type of springy tissue. Cartilage keeps bones from rubbing together.

contracts (kun-TRAKTS) When something contracts, it gets tighter. A muscle contracts to bend an arm.

glands (GLANDZ) Glands produce and give off chemicals in the body. Glands produce sweat.

ligaments (LIG-uh-muhnts) Ligaments are firm tissues that connect bones. Ligaments hold bones together.

nutrients (NOO-tree-unts) Nutrients are what living things need to stay healthy. Blood carries nutrients.

sensitive (SEN-suh-tiv) Being sensitive is noticing small feelings. Skin is sensitive.

socket (SOK-it) A socket is an opening where a ball can fit. Hip joints move like a ball in a socket.

tendons (TEN-duhnz) Tendons are firm tissues that connect muscles and bones. Tendons attach to a bone on one end and a muscle on the other.

TO LEARN MORE

IN THE LIBRARY

Columbo, Luann. *Inside Out Human Body*. Bellevue, WA: becker&mayer!, 2017.

Dickmann, Nancy. *Q & A about the Human Body*. New York, NY: PowerKids Press, 2018.

Midthun, Joseph. *Cells to Organ Systems*. Chicago, IL: World Book, 2014.

ON THE WEB

Visit our website for links about the human body:

childsworld.com/links